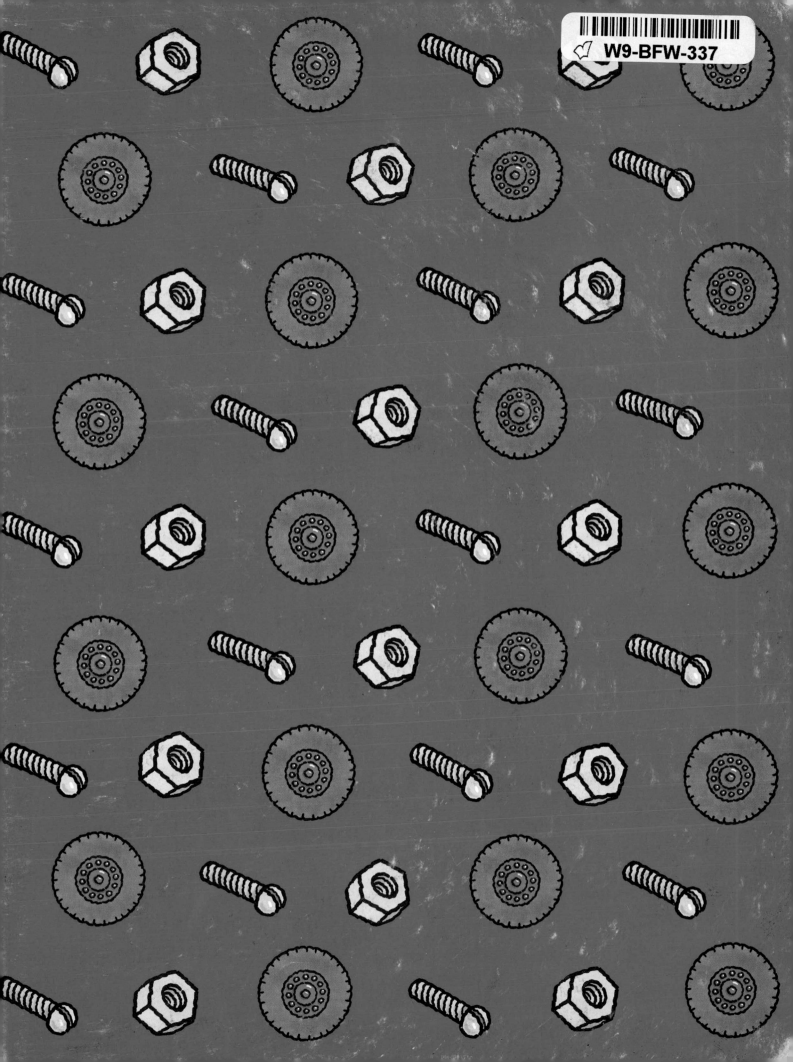

A DK PUBLISHING BOOK

Editor Mary Ling
Designer Mike Buckley
Managing Editor Sheila Hanly
US Editor Camela Decaire
Production Josie Alabaster
Photography Richard Leeney
Illustrator Derek Matthews

First American edition, 1996
2 4 6 8 10 9 7 5 3

Published in the United States by
DK Publishing, Inc.,
95 Madison Avenue, New York, New York 10016

A CIP catalog record is available from the
Library of Congress.
ISBN: 0-7894-0574-1

Color reproduction by Chromagraphics, Singapore
Printed and bound in Italy by L.E.G.O.

DK would like to thank: Paul Gammons,
Lisa Smart and Steve Warner of the Blue Blazer Racing
team (dragster), Henry J. Gracia at Chris Hodge (racing
truck), all at Malcolm Wilson Motorsport (rally car), and
Nicky Marsh and Marcus Potts at Marcos Cars (Le Mans)
for all their help and advice.

The publisher would like to thank the following for their kind
permission to reproduce their photographs:
l left, r right, t top, c center, a above, b below.

Allsport/Howard Boylan 4cr,12/13c;/Mike Cooper 5c, 8/9c,
9tr;/Ken Levine 19tl;/Anton Want 13tr; Ray Archer
10c,11bl; Autosport 6/7b; Renault Communication 4t, 7tr.

Every effort has been made to trace the copyright
holders and we apologize in advance for any
unintentional omissions. We would be pleased to
insert the appropriate acknowledgment in any
subsequent edition of this publication.

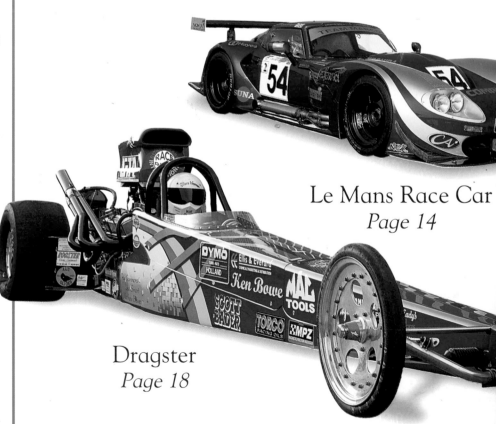

Mighty Machines

RACE CAR

Caroline Bingham

Motocross Bike
Page 10

Sidecar Racer
Page 12

Grand Prix Motorcycle
Page 8

Rally Car
Page 20

DK

Formula 1

AMAZING FACTS

An average car could take you around the world in 16 days. A Formula 1 could whisk you around in just five – if it didn't stop!

Formula 1 cars line up in two rows on a starting grid and a race begins. The cars have 187 miles (300 km) to go before the race finishes, all on a race circuit only about three miles (five km) in length. Each car is built low to the ground to help it cut through the air and turn corners as fast as possible. It is an exciting sight!

roll bar protects the driver in an accident

air duct

Air is sucked into the car through **air ducts** to help cool the engine.

A tight fit

The driver sits in a small cockpit in front of the engine – so small that the steering wheel is added after the driver climbs in!

engine fills all the space behind the driver

cockpit

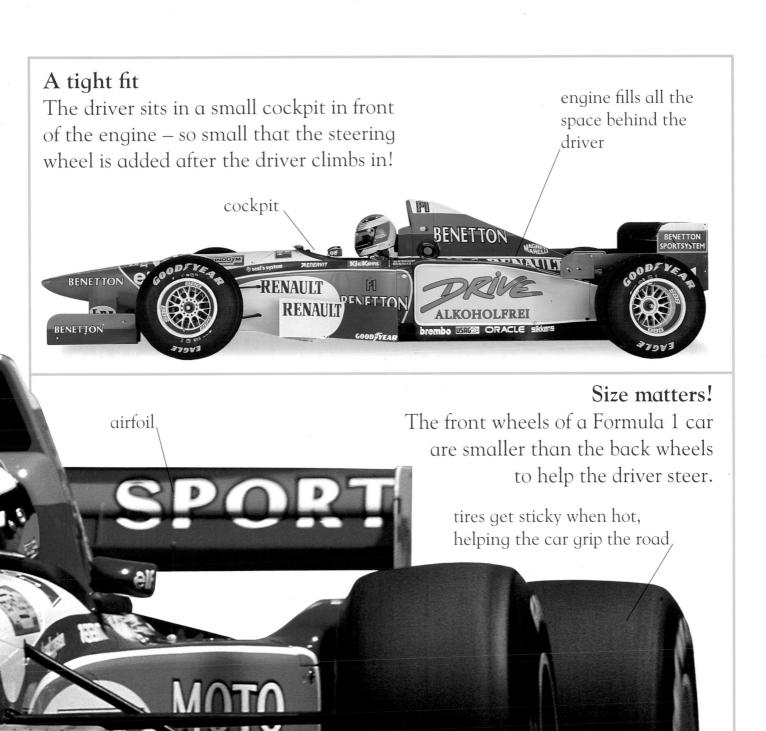

Size matters!

The front wheels of a Formula 1 car are smaller than the back wheels to help the driver steer.

airfoil

tires get sticky when hot, helping the car grip the road

The car's front and rear **airfoils** act like upside-down airplane wings.

Grand Prix Motorcycle

Grand Prix motorcycles zoom their riders along at incredible speeds. The bikes race in classes according to their engine size and power, either 125 cc, 250 cc, or 500 cc – the most powerful class of all Grand Prix bikes.

rider is well protected in leather suit

rider uses foot rests

motorcycles have powerful front and rear wheel brakes

rider's knee is well protected by nylon "sliders"

  cc (cubic centimeter) is a measurement of engine size and power.

A flick of the wrist

Motorcycle riders control their machines with their hands and feet. They twist a throttle on the handlebars to make the engine go faster and pull levers to work the brakes.

rider leans low

Front view

Over we go!

The rider has to lean into a bend with the bike. If he or she tried to sit upright, the bike would slide into a crash.

Back view

AMAZING FACTS

Grand Prix racing bikes are powerful – easily as powerful as 170 horses all pulling together.

A Grand Prix bike can accelerate to the speed limit on a highway faster than you can jump up and down five times.

A **throttle** on the handlebars controls the bike's speed and acceleration.

Motocross Bike

Motocross riders take their bikes over mud, ice, and snow, up and down hills, and through streams. The bikes are specially made for this rough treatment and look very different from other racing bikes.

helmet has a filter to keep out dust

knobby tires help bike grip the ground

Tires are made of rubber and fit around a wheel rim.

A cushioned ride

Special springs at the front and back of a motocross bike help cushion the worst effects of a bumpy ride. This is the bike's suspension system.

handlebars

long seat lets the rider move around

engine high off the ground

shock absorber

Up we go!

Motocross bikes sometimes leave the ground as the rider accelerates over the top of a hill.

rider leans forward in the air

rider leans back on landing

AMAZING FACTS

A motocross bike's suspension lets the wheels move up and down by about one foot (30 cm).

Motocross bikes have high seats. At about 3 ft (one meter) from the ground, they are a lot taller than other racing bikes.

A motocross bike's engine clears the ground by 13 in (33 cm).

 Shock absorbers are like strong springs, and compress to cushion bumps.

Sidecar Racer

Some motorcycles have a sidecar for a passenger to sit in, but sidecar racers are more like small, powerful cars than motorcycles. A passenger in this machine has to constantly adjust his or her position to balance the bike and increase its speed. The sidecars have special knee channels and grips for the passenger's use.

the driver and passenger stay low

a fairing, or panel, covers the front and sides of the racer

aerodynamic shape

Aerodynamic shapes are curved to slide through the air.

We have takeoff!

On corners, the sidecar's tire can leave the ground. The passenger has to lean out to stop the whole racer from tipping over.

passenger uses hand grips to stay on board

motorcycle and sidecar have three tires

AMAZING FACTS

The first sidecars were simply made. They were basically motorcyles with chairs bolted onto the sides.

Sidecar racers can speed around a corner faster than a Grand Prix motorcycle because they have three tires. This means more rubber is touching the race track.

 The **fairing** smooths the sidecar racer's shape, helping it cut through the air.

Le Mans Race Car

AMATING FACTS

Le Mans cars travel 3000 mi (4830 km) in 24 hours. This would take 41 days to walk nonstop!

A Le Mans car competes in a race that lasts 24 hours at a place called Le Mans, in France. It is a long time to race nonstop, and three drivers have to take turns driving the car for two or three hours each. The race is a test of a car's endurance.

One lap of the Le Mans circuit takes the car only four minutes.

exhaust pipes run along each side of the car

each wheel is held on by only one nut

A strong metal **nut** is screwed in place to hold a car's wheels in position.

drivers constantly look for a chance to overtake any cars in front

Is it sunny today?

The tires used for races depend on the weather. If it's dry, a smooth, "slick" tire will be used. If it rains, grooved wet-weather tires replace the slicks.

Wet   Dry

air sucked in here helps cool the engine

towing eye

Racing Truck

This racing truck has the same power as 1,300 horses! As the driver revs up, the engine roars. The race starts and the truck thunders off down the race circuit at twice the speed limit allowed on a normal road.

large guards cover rear wheels

the six tires are replaced before each race

this step is used to climb up into the cab

  The **hood** is the metal cover over the engine that can be opened up.

Let's go!

A special semitrailer carries the racing truck and extra supplies to and from races.

extra tires and replacement parts are stored here

a mesh net protects the driver

hood

AMAZING FACTS

Trucks are heavy! This racing truck weighs 5.5 tons (5 tonnes) – that's as heavy as 201 seven-year-old children.

Racing trucks guzzle fuel. This truck needs ten times the fuel an ordinary car does to cover the same distance.

A standard car travels 25 miles per gallon.

there are headlights and turn signals, just like an ordinary truck

Dragster

Two dragsters line up, back wheels spinning. The starting lights flash to green and the cars shoot off down a drag strip. In little more than five seconds the cars release parachutes and the race is over. They have only traveled 1/4 mile (400 meters).

Back view of dragster

exhaust pipe

driver wears a fireproof suit, a neck brace, and a helmet

parachute is kept in a small bag

long, slim body, streamlined for speed

dragsters are usually brightly colored

  Streamlined means something is shaped to glide through the air.

Burning out

The driver spins the back wheels before a race to heat them up. Besides making the tires sticky, it makes a lot of noise and causes lots of smoke.

air duct

front wheels are smaller than back wheels

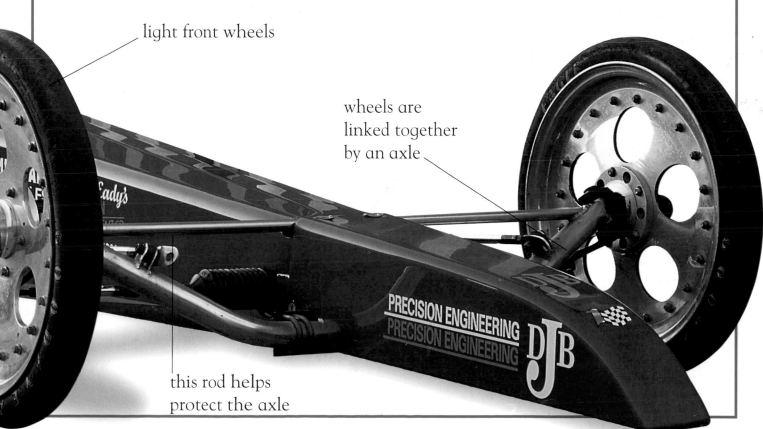

light front wheels

wheels are linked together by an axle

this rod helps protect the axle

An **axle** is a metal rod that connects a set of wheels.

Rally Car

Rally car races often take place over several days. A driver and a navigator follow a course that will take them along not only roads, but cross-country on deeply rutted dirt tracks or worse!

vent allows air to circulate inside the car

rear wing improves tire grip

mud flap

Where are we now?
Rally cars pass through forests and on up into icy mountains in the course of a four-day rally. Navigators must be good map readers.

Large **mud flaps** help protect the car from stones kicked up by the wheels.

An ordinary car?

A rally car may look like a car you've seen on the road, but it is very different, with an enormous fuel tank, strong roll bars, and wheels that can be changed in seconds.

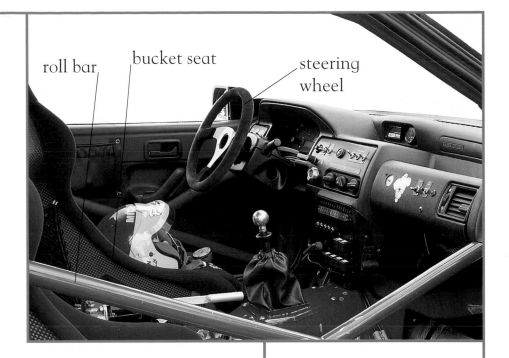

roll bar

bucket seat

steering wheel

heated windshield to keep mist and ice from forming

spotlights for night driving

AMAZING FACTS

In a typical four-day rally, a rally car will go through about 120 tires. These are carried on a support vehicle.

The car uses different tires for different conditions – the tires even vary in width. Ice tires have metal spikes to grip the ground.

M10 MWM

bar to hold lights steady

pins hold hood down at high speed

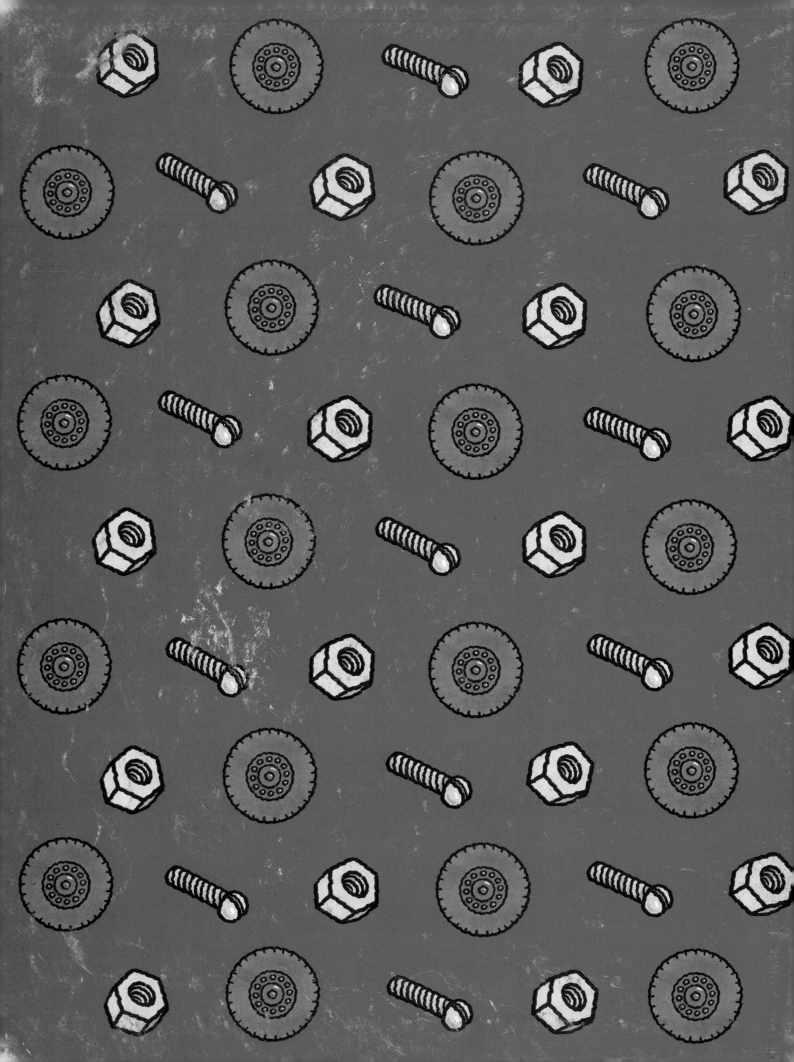